Manifestation Using Crystals

Applying Crystal Energy, The Law of Attraction and
Intention, Through a Unique Process to Obtain Your Desires

By

Debbie Hardy

ISBN: 9781696991391

Debbie Hardy © 2019
Cover Image by Elisa Lee

Disclaimer

The author is not a medical practitioner, cannot give medical or psychological advice or diagnose patients, and cannot prescribe medications. Please consult your licensed medical practitioner if you have any health or psychological concerns. The information provided in this book is not a substitute for medical, legal, or other expert advice. Please be advised there are no guarantees that the following content will heal your specific situation, and there are no guarantees of specific results from following the guidance of this book. Information provided in this book is as accurate as possible; however, the author accepts no responsibility or liability for any loss or damage caused by the information given in this book.

Other Books by Debbie Hardy

Meditation Made Easy Using Crystals

If you have struggled with meditation or had difficulty clearing the chatter in your head, this is a must-read book for you. It also explains how to work on self-healing, connection to angels, and deeper soul connection by using crystals during meditation. It is geared toward all levels of meditation experience. The book provides a healing layout that you can do on your own, as well as a guided meditation—plus so much more!

"I would highly recommend this beautiful book to those just beginning with crystals, to those who want to review, or [to those who want to] get a different point of view [on using] crystals in practical meditation or in general life use. Debbie speaks with a clarity of voice that is easy to [relate to]. I could easily follow along with her writing style, and nothing felt jarring to me as I read. I found practical advice I'd like to incorporate into my daily wellness practice, as well as new information about high-vibration crystals that I'd love to explore. Very well done!" ~ Nightingeal

"I absolutely loved Debbie's book. It was easy to follow, and it even had a diagram of how [to] line your crystals to rid yourself of negative energy. The feeling was so wonderful. Afterward I followed the instructions to bring in the positive energy. It was awesome! I highly recommend it." ~ Mina

"I thoroughly enjoyed reading this book, because I have tried meditation in the past and was unable to meditate on my own. There was too much 'chatter' in my head, or I was influenced by outside distractions, or I couldn't set the proper mood…the list of excuses is endless. So I tried books. This list is also endless. Other books made meditation seem mysterious and complicated—to me, anyway. But here the author has demystified the practice of meditation, made it uncomplicated, and enhanced it with the use of crystals! I am still a beginner and may never reach the author's level of expertise, but one thing is for sure: this is not a book I will put down or put away. In fact, I have already started reading it for the second time! I have now been able to relax, de-stress, unwind, and not take everything so seriously. Plus, I have started my own collection of crystals. Thank you, Debbie Hardy, for all you've taught me!" ~ Carol

Spirit of the Crystal Ray

This is a twenty-one-day guide of channeled guidance from spirit to help you with your journey. Learn what spirit feels is important to focus on now at this point in your life. This is a sublime journey into the crystal ray to enlightenment, self-discovery, self-healing, and personal growth. Be prepared to experience divine love, beauty, and grace for yourself.

"Spirit speaks to us [through] Debbie Hardy in a compassionate, understandable way that touched me deeply. The lessons shared are universal in scope. Spirit wants only for our true happiness and shares how to achieve this. Highly recommend this book for anyone searching for truth and love made visible." ~ Paula

"Just finished your new book yesterday—WOW. I absolutely loved it! I've learned so much [and] it felt like I was gifted all the gold in the world and hugged and loved unconditionally. Thank you, Thank you, Thank you!" ~ Michele

"I could not put this book down. I believe it really captured me on Day 5. After that there were other days that stuck out more so, but the way Debbie Hardy was able to make me feel as if I was entering the cave with her was what kept me going back eagerly to see what the next journey would be and where it would take us. I am looking forward to another one of your journeys, this book has brought home an understanding that although I have heard many things said in so many ways on my journey, they were not nearly as clear as the messages I felt as I heard Debbie's message. I know that this book will serve me well many times over, good job, Debbie." ~ Suzan

I dedicate this book to the alchemist within you.

Contents

Introduction

Manifestation is important for many people. We all wish to do, achieve, or obtain something we do not currently have. When we are in alignment (balanced) with positive energy, the components of what we ask for start to fall into place. If we are out of alignment, the energy is blocked and there is no flow. Based on years of observation and experience with the law of attraction and working with crystal energy, I have created a step-by-step process that reduces the negative so that the positive can flow in. When you incorporate the law of attraction with setting intentions and the use of crystal energy to enhance the intentions you set, you create an amazing positive energy flow that amplifies the process.

When your body, mind, and spirit are completely aligned, it is easy to manifest what you want. Have you ever known someone who obtains whatever it is that they want with ease? It is because they have an inner knowing that it can be accomplished effortlessly; they know without question. They are in alignment with their body, mind, and spirit.

Reducing and eliminating the negative allows the positive to flow in. However, it takes practice. If you are continually stuck in a negative cycle, it can take some time and practice to break free from that cycle. The more you hold and maintain the positive, the more the things that you hope for will occur. It is our goal here to reduce and eliminate the negative and to allow the positive to flow in order for you to manifest your desires.

In addition to my experiences, many of my community members have had great success using this process. For the universe to respond to your request, it depends on how you ask for something as well as the emotional state you are in at the time. It can take time for some requests to occur, but if you go through each phase of the process, you should begin to see positive changes within your life regardless of what you ask for. Take the time to follow the phases of reducing negative energy to allow for positive energy to flow to you. It can make a big difference. When energy flows easily, things fall into place quickly.

My Experience

Several years ago, I was in a negative vibration. My thoughts were consumed with negativity, worry, and fear, and I suffered from a complete sense of lack. My family was in a financial crisis, my health was poor, and I was experiencing many emotional, mental, and physical issues. My husband was out of work, and my paycheck was not enough to cover all the bills. I felt as though I was at an all-time low in my life.

One day something clicked within me, and I finally decided that things needed to change. I began incorporating many positive practices into my daily life. Some of those included changing my thought process to try to turn the negative thoughts into positive thoughts on a daily basis. That in itself is not an easy task, but it is well worth it. I also incorporated gratitude exercises, daily meditation, and working with crystal energy, and I focused on my own inner well-being. That is when things started to change for the better. To name just a few benefits, I became more inspired, energetic, healthy, and peaceful in a short amount of time by practicing these daily rituals. More opportunities began flowing to me without effort. Doors began to open that had been shut before. It truly was a transformation.

Now I am at a completely different place in my life. I have manifested countless things since I began these practices and have maintained a more positive vibration. I believe that I had to experience what I did in order to learn from it and teach others how to help themselves in similar ways. In the following pages, I will share many of the practices I used to help pull myself out of a negative space and transform it into a positive space. This change in mind-set will help you to manifest what you want. When your energy is in alignment (balanced), you will see that things occur and flow to you more easily than when you are out of alignment. First you have to clear the negative to allow the positive to come into your being.

The Law of Attraction and Crystal Energy

I am a big believer in the law of attraction. To pull myself out of the negative state I was in, I began using the law of attraction with my positive thought process. Briefly, the law of attraction states that like attracts like. If you have a positive thought, then positive things will occur, and if you have a negative thought, then negative things will occur. I have been using my own practices of incorporating crystal energy with the law of attraction for several years now, and I continue to see results. I believe that there are several critical components to acquiring what you want that tend to be overlooked at times, so I created a unique system that incorporates crystal energy within each phase of the manifestation process, which allows manifestation to occur. Yes, you get what you think about, so keep your thoughts positive. That's easier said than done, right? It does work with practice, but I believe there is more to it than that. We have to clear out the negative in order to allow the positive to flow to us. Although I have incorporated crystal energy suggestions into each component of the manifestation process, it is not required to use crystals to achieve results. I have had several clients use this system without crystal energy and they had great success in doing so. However, crystal energy enhances and amplifies the process, so I urge you to give it a try. I have used crystals for several years now in many aspects of my daily life, even the manifestation process, and I have found that crystal energy does assist in what I am trying to achieve or obtain. In each chapter, I will suggest crystals to use and will guide you on how to incorporate those crystals into that part of the process.

Because we are all different and because everyone will approach each chapter of the book in various ways, I cannot guarantee specific results for everyone. I do believe, however, that if you follow the guidance and suggestions described on the following pages that you will begin to notice many positive changes within your life. By releasing the negative and allowing the positive to flow in, that allows the positive energy of manifestation to occur. I encourage you to keep an open mind and to attempt to work through the phases at your own pace. Do not try to rush it and accomplish it all in one sitting. Give yourself time to heal what needs to be healed, to release what needs to be released, and trust that you are allowing yourself to be open to receiving what you wish for.

When you think of the word *manifestation*, what does it mean to you? Manifestation means to materialize something. So many people focus their intentions to manifest money. If that is what you'd like to manifest, I suggest that you think of it a bit differently. What would you want to manifest if money were not a factor? What object(s), or occurrence(s), do you wish for? I have included a chapter on creating an abundance/prosperity grid that will cover the money component after you set your intention for what you want to manifest; this is an added benefit of the whole process. I encourage you to think of something other than money.

You can focus your intention on whatever it is you want to manifest. Some of the more common areas are love or relationships, jobs or careers, material objects (such as a car or home), travel, peace and harmony, or health and well-being. It is completely up to you.

Using Crystal Energy

I have provided a list of recommended crystals to use throughout the manifestation process. Although crystals are not required and many clients have used this process successfully without crystals, it is my experience that bringing in crystal energy can enhance and elevate the experience of releasing negative energy, allowing positive energy to flow in and setting intentions when you are going through the manifestation process. If you choose to work with crystals, select one or more for each part of the process. For example, to release fear, select one of the following: red jasper, garnet, or ruby. You will not need all three to achieve the reduction of fear, although if you choose to work with more than one in a particular category, you may do so. Use your intuition to lead you to the crystal best suited to your energy for each phase. This is not a comprehensive list of crystals to choose from for the various phases of the process. Instead, I have listed crystals that I have worked with successfully, and they are generally less expensive and easily obtainable in the tumbled form.

I want to touch briefly on the topic of crystal energy before we get started. How does crystal energy work? Crystal energy entrains with our energy. If our energy is out of alignment, such as being in a negative state of mind, and we bring crystal energy into our energy field, then our energy will become like that of the crystal's energy because the crystal's energy is typically more stable than ours. Hibiscus Moon describes it as "our energy is becoming in sync with the crystal energy...it is actually bringing us closer to its vibrational frequency."[1] For example, if we are feeling insecure and unsure about money, we can work with a specific crystal to reduce those fears in order to clear the negative vibrations that we hold, which then allows our energy field to become like that of the crystal. That is how we become balanced. When we become balanced, positive things begin to flow to us.

By holding or placing crystals around our energy field during the suggested phases of the process, I have found that it provides quicker results than doing so without crystal energy. In addition, you receive the specific attributes associated with the selected crystal you use during the process.

Cleansing Crystals

If you decide to use crystals during this process, you will want to cleanse and clear them first. Some quick ways to cleanse your crystals include water, sage, sound, and moonlight. Use the method that you prefer and that works best for you. Cleansing and clearing the crystals you use often allows them to reset their energy to continue to provide the best possible results in working with them.

Most tumbled or polished crystals can be rinsed off with water. However, some will flake and break down. Check the Mohs hardness scale (Google "Mohs hardness for crystal [INSERT CRYSTAL NAME]"), and if it says 7 or above, then it is safe to place in water for cleansing. All the crystals on the crystal list should be fine rinsed under water for a few minutes, except lepidolite and selenite.

---

[1] "Crystals for Grounding, Prosperity, Drip Stone, and What Is Entrainment?," Hibiscus Moon, Hibiscus Moon Crystal Academy, accessed August 20, 2019, https://hibiscusmooncrystalacademy.com/grounding-prosperity.

If you are unsure of the water method, you can sage smudge your crystals. Light a bundle of sage and blow out the flame, being sure to be fire safe. The smoke of the sage will cleanse, clear, and reset the crystal's energy. Let the smoke of the sage drift over your crystals for a moment with the intention of cleansing and clearing their energy. Be sure to completely extinguish the sage smudge carefully after use.

Another method for cleansing and clearing crystal energy is sound. Singing bowls, tingsha bells, or drums are excellent choices of sound source to cleanse crystal energy. Just play the sound near the crystals you choose to work with for a few moments.

Crystals love full moon energy as well. Place your crystals under the full moon light and notice how refreshed they feel the next morning.

You should cleanse the crystals you use often to reset their energy so that they will provide optimum results. Many people tend to over think the cleansing process. Do not stress over it—and rely on your intuition too!

Optimal Manifestation Times

There are a few times a year when universal energies are optimal for setting intentions. You do not have to wait for one of these times, but I wanted you to be aware of them in case you decide to take advantage of the added benefit of these time periods.

Within the moon cycle, the new moon is a good time to set intentions. Like the new moon, intentions grow from that point forward. You can plan to work through the phases of manifestation around a new moon cycle during any month.

The seasons resemble the manifestation process. The spring equinox is an excellent time to plant the seeds of manifestation. The summer solstice is when you see signs and indications that things are growing and moving forward. The fall equinox is the harvest season and the time to reap the rewards of the seeds you planted. The winter solstice is a time for planning the next cycle. You do not have to wait for all the seasons, and the manifestation cycle does not follow the exact timeline of the season, but the cycle itself mimics the seasons. However, the spring equinox displays a heightened energy for intention setting.

The Lion's Gate of August 8 is a powerful portal of energy. The Lion's Gate is when the sun is in Leo and it is synced with the star Sirius.[2] It occurs on August 8, and the number eight resembles infinity, manifestation, and abundance. This is when we are given insight and guidance, and it is an excellent time to set intentions. I set manifestation intentions each year during Lion's Gate, and the energy is powerful and positive; I have seen amazing results very quickly during this period of time.

The start of a new year is also an excellent time to set intentions. It is a fresh new year and offers fresh energy and a fresh start. It does not have to be on New Year's Day, but you can plan it shortly thereafter if your goal is to set intentions during this time of year.

---

[2] "Lion's Gate: The Sun and Sirius Sync Up to Open a Powerful Portal on 8-8," Felicia Bender, Astrostyle.com, accessed August 20, 2019, https://astrostyle.com/lions-gate-portal.

As mentioned before, you do not have to wait for these specific times to set your wish or intention requests, but the energies surrounding these times are an added benefit of doing so. Go ahead with the process now, and when we get to those times during the year, set another intention.

Other Information

When I speak of the universe, this includes but is not limited to God, creator, source energy, higher power, spirit guides, or any other higher power of your understanding.

Throughout, the book will use terms like *request, wish, intention,* and *prayer.* I use these terms interchangeably because everyone has their own preference for the specific practice.

This process can take time and effort. How much effort you put into it determines how quickly you will see results. If you have been consumed with negative energy for years, it can take time to release and heal that. If it took years to get to that point, it will take a bit of time to adjust your energies. However, once you begin the process, regardless of how long you have been stuck in a negative cycle, you should start to notice positive changes right away. You may need to repeat certain phases before you receive the full effects of positive flow back to you. You will know when you are ready to move on. Each phase builds on the previous one, so it is important that you follow the phases in order to achieve the best desired outcome. During the manifestation process, keep in mind that some prayers, requests, and intentions take time to manifest while other requests can occur rather quickly. Some of my intentions have manifested within days and weeks after setting the intention while other requests took several months for the final outcome to occur.

Each chapter includes suggested exercises and/or journaling prompts, so if you have a favorite journal, please use that or a notebook. I encourage you to try the suggestions listed for each phase to get the most out of it.

I am so excited that you are joining me on this journey of manifestation, and I wish you success and abundance along the way.

Are you ready to get started on the manifestation journey?

Crystals and Other Supplies

You will not need all the crystals listed for each phase. Choose one or more from each category to work with during the corresponding phase. I suggest that you use the tumbled form (unless otherwise stated) because they are easily obtainable and easy to hold and work with.

- Releasing negative energy (depending on what your main issue is)
  o Releasing doubt, fear, and insecurities: red jasper, garnet, petrified wood, or ruby
  o Releasing negative energy in general, blocks and limitations, and blocking negative energy: black tourmaline, obsidian, hematite, shungite, or smoky quartz
- Finding your joy: citrine, aventurine, emerald, carnelian, ocean jasper, or jade
- Expressing gratitude: rose quartz
- Focusing on your intention: fluorite, clear quartz, or sodalite
- Maintaining a positive vibration: clear quartz, emerald, citrine, pyrite, or sunstone
- Stating your intention: citrine, emerald, jade, clear quartz, tiger eye, pyrite, carnelian or green aventurine
- The power trio: citrine, green aventurine, and pyrite
- Sending blessings: rose quartz

- Using an abundance grid:
  - Tumbled stones: citrine, emerald, jade, clear quartz, pyrite, tiger eye, or green aventurine
  - Point: clear quartz
  - Wand: clear quartz or selenite
- Open and allowing: labradorite and prehnite
- Trust and believe: amethyst, clear quartz, labradorite, or sodalite
- Signs and indications: clear quartz, selenite, sodalite, or labradorite
- Time and patience: lepidolite, moonstone, selenite, angelite, or amethyst

Other optional items include the following:
- Journal or notebook
- Sage bundle
- Palo santo stick
- Essential oils: peppermint, sage, lavender, myrrh, frankincense, or oil of your choice
- Incense: nag champa, frankincense, sandalwood, palo santo, cedarwood, lavender, rosemary, or your choice
- Aroma spray: sage, lavender, or your choice
- Glass or ceramic dish or abalone shell

Releasing Negative Energy

Like many people, I have been stuck in negative cycles during periods of my life. I know how hard it is to get out of those cycles, and sometimes it feels like that is all there is. Several years back, I was in a negative cycle during which I was consumed with worry, fear, insecurity, and an overall feeling of lack. After years of being in that cycle, I finally decided to change my thought process and my daily practices. I began releasing the negative and allowing the positive to flow in. With daily meditation using crystals, I began noticing in just a short amount of time that I was at a much more peaceful state than I had been in many years. I started sleeping better, worrying less, and letting go of negative thoughts that previously consumed my mind. Once I was able to release the negative and allow the positive to flow in, my life began to change. Things that I used to think were unobtainable began happening effortlessly and easily. This did not happen all at once, and it has been an ongoing process, but as soon as I released the negative energy that consumed me, my life quickly began to change for the better.

Releasing negative energy (fear, doubt, anger, sadness, frustration, etc.) is the first key component of the manifestation process. We will concentrate on releasing manifestation blocks and limiting beliefs. By releasing negative energies, we allow positive energies to flow in. I have found that if you set your intentions or ask for something in a positive manner, it is much more likely to occur or manifest. If we set our intentions or ask for what we want to manifest while we are under distress of any kind, we will block the energy from flowing. The suggestions in the following paragraphs will help you to release negative energy. Try what resonates with you. If some do not seem to be helping much, try the other suggestions until you find one that works best for you. The goal is to clear all negative energies so that you are in a more positive energy vibration in order to increase your energy flow for when you set your intention for your manifestation request.

The following are some crystals that I like to work with to reduce or release fears, self-limiting beliefs, negative thoughts, insecurities, and negative energies in general. You do not need all these crystals, but I wanted to give you a selection from which to choose. Select one or more that you feel is right for you and hold it during each phase of your releasing exercises. Red jasper, garnet, petrified wood, and ruby are effective for reducing fears and insecurities. Black tourmaline, obsidian, smoky quartz, shungite, and hematite are effective for reducing and/or blocking negative energy from a person or space.

There are many things that can block the manifestation process. These can include but are not limited to fears, self-doubts or doubting beliefs in general, negative thoughts, negative emotions (such as sadness, anger, frustration, impatience, or limiting beliefs), lack of concentration, lack of confidence, or any other negative or limiting energies you may be holding on to. By releasing these negative energies, we open the flow for positive energies to enter our body, mind, and spirit. When we request, ask, pray, or set intentions for things we want to obtain, do, or manifest, it is best do so while in a positive mind-set. If we are thinking or feeling negative energies when we ask for something, it is less likely to occur. If you say, for instance, "I really want that job, but I know I will not get it," what do you think will happen? If you request something and you are holding on to feelings of anger, sadness, or any other negative energy, in return you get more of the same. It is the law of attraction.

Most likely you will not get what you requested because of the negative energies you are holding on to and emitting. We will practice releasing exercises that you can use anytime you feel that you need to release the negative energy and bring in the flow of positive energy. I have listed several ways to reduce or eliminate negative energy in the following pages, so choose what works best for you or try to combine several of them to achieve optimum results.

Journaling

Journaling is an excellent way to release energies that are holding you back or if you are feeling strong negative emotions, such as anger, fear, sadness, or even pain.

Take a few moments for yourself and sit down with a journal (if you don't have a journal, use a pen and paper). Select one of the suggested crystals for this chapter and hold it while you write in your journal. Find a quiet place to sit where you will not be disturbed, and put your electronics away. When you begin your journaling, think about what you want to release and what feelings or emotions are prominent in your life right now. Write what caused them. If you do not know what caused them, write how you feel about the situation. Just let the words flow on the paper, and do not worry about spelling, punctuation, or formatting. For example, maybe you were stuck in traffic, which caused you a lot of stress, anger, and impatience, and maybe that occurrence has caused you to hold on to some of those feelings. Perhaps you got home and the anger was so apparent that you lashed out at a family member or maybe you were just feeling unsettled overall. Write down all the details of the situation, where you were, the time of day, where you were trying to go, and all the instances that caused the stressful situation. Write down exactly how you feel or felt at the time.

When I experience challenging times in my life, I typically go outside where it is quiet and just start writing and writing. I have found that when I start writing and I let it flow, more and more pages are filled with all I am feeling. This is an alternative way to release, especially if you do not feel like talking to someone or if you do not have someone to talk to. You can talk to the pages by writing. When I finish, I always feel lighter and have less tension than when I started the process.

When you are done, take a deep breath in and just let it go. You can tear up your pages and throw them away or leave them in the journal if you prefer. Go with how you feel about it. Give it a try. You may be surprised by how you feel after writing your emotions down.

Using Plant-Based Energy

Crystal energy works very well with plant energy. They tend to complement each other, so choose one or more of the releasing crystals you wish to work with and then decide which type of plant-based energy you would like to try.

Consider incorporating aromatherapy into your releasing experience. This is a type of treatment using extracts from plants called essential oils, by either breathing them in through your nose or putting them on your skin. If you have an oil diffuser, you can add your favorite oil to that and place it in a space where you can sit and relax for a bit. Explore the many different types of essential oils available and use what resonates with you. Be sure to look at the usage label before applying directly to your skin because some could cause irritation. Some essential oils that I suggest to reduce negative energy are peppermint, sage, lavender, myrrh, or frankincense, but you can use any that you are drawn to.

Sage smudging is also highly effective in releasing negative energy. White sage is popular, and there are several varieties available on the market. They all have a slightly different scent, so try a few to see which ones you like best. To sage smudge, you will need a ceramic or glass dish or abalone shell and a sage bundle. If you are doing this inside, be aware that the smoke may cause the smoke alarm to go off, and please remember to always be fire safe. Light the sage bundle and blow out the flame. It is the smoke of the sage that clears the energy. If you are sage smudging the space you are in, start at one area of the room and walk in a clockwise direction, brushing the smoke in all areas of the room. You can open the windows and doors to let the smoke flow out. Use the dish or shell to catch any embers that may fall. State or think such intentions as "I release all negative energy in this space," or something along those lines, as you smudge the space.

You can also sage smudge yourself after a stressful day or if you just need to release any harboring negative energy. I typically do this after I have had a stressful day at work, have been stuck in traffic for a long time, or even after visiting family in the hospital. When I smudge myself, I typically stand outside, and it takes only a few minutes. After lighting the sage bundle and blowing out the flame, and you can either wave it around your body from bottom to top and front and back, or you can place the smoking smudge stick in the dish or shell at your feet and let the smoke drift around you. If you are sitting in a space or meditating, you can let the smoke from the sage float freely around you while it sits in the shell or dish. Be sure to extinguish the sage when you are finished.

Every time I use sage smudging, I notice a difference in the energy right away and I feel so much lighter and free of tension and stress almost immediately.

Palo santo sticks, also known as holy wood, reduce negative energy the same way as sage. Light the stick and blow out the flame. This is similar to sage because it is the smoke that provides the release of negative energy. Palo santo sticks can be hard to light and keep lit, so you may have to get a good flame started before you blow it out. Then you would use it the same way as the sage.

Burning incense is another option. There are many choices for incense, so try a few to see what resonates with you. Some good choices for releasing negative energy are nag champa, frankincense, sandalwood, palo santo, cedarwood, lavender, or rosemary, but again, use one that you like. It is a good idea to have an incense holder, either for cone or stick incense. Light the incense and let the smoke of the incense drift over you.

For those who are sensitive to smoke, try using a sage or lavender aroma spray. Spray yourself or the area prior to your clearing session. There are many variations of sprays available, so be sure to use one that smells good to you.

Connecting to Nature

Connecting to nature is an excellent way to reduce or eliminate negative energies. Select one of the crystals that you would like to work with and hold it. If do not have a lot of time, try going for a walk to clear your head. As you do, try to focus on what is around you and how you feel being outdoors in the fresh air. You can also sit outside awhile. Find a quiet place to just sit for a bit of time. Perhaps you could go to your favorite nature spot: a garden in your backyard, a walk along the beach or among the trees in the mountains, the desert, or any other place in nature that you prefer. Sit awhile in that space and take in all that surrounds you. Remember to breathe! When we are faced with negative issues or emotions, we tend to hold our breath. Wherever it is that you choose, go outside in nature and take some deep breaths. Fill your lungs with fresh air and notice how you feel after doing that a few times. Whatever place you decide on, listen to what you hear, and look at all the beauty that surrounds you. Whether you are sitting, or walking, be in the moment, appreciate all that is around you, and just be.

I love the beach and ocean, but when I cannot get to there, I like to sit in my backyard and look at the plants, birds, and lizards. I listen to all the sounds that are in that moment of time. It is always so relaxing to connect with nature. It does not have to be a long, drawn-out process. Just find somewhere you can go to be in nature for a few minutes and focus on being in the moment with all that surrounds you. Notice how you feel after you connect with nature. Do you feel less anxious, tense, or stressed?

Meditation

Meditation can eliminate negative energies and bring you to a deeper state of peace rather quickly, especially if you do it often. Daily meditation with crystals has completely changed my life. Once I started using crystals in my daily meditation ritual, I became more at peace almost immediately. Then other things began to change in a short amount of time. I worried less, I had less fear overall, I began to sleep better and more soundly, and I felt more energetic and happier during the day. Meditation is worth every moment you put into it.

The easiest way to meditate with crystals is to hold your selected crystal and either sit or lie down for a bit of time. Take a few deep breaths in and out and relax your body. Focus on the energy of the crystal you are holding to keep thoughts from consuming your mind. If a thought comes to mind, gently let it go and refocus on the crystal you are holding and feel its healing energy. Visualize the energy from the crystal you are holding encompassing you in a beautiful bubble of radiant, positive light, and feel the energy that surrounds you as you do so. You can add some quiet meditative music or even a guided meditation to help with the process if you struggle with meditation. Try to meditate for at least ten to twenty minutes or more, and when you are finished, notice how you are feeling. If you would like more assistance with the meditative process, check out my book *Meditation Made Easy Using Crystals.*[3]

If you do not want to take the time for a full meditation session, you can do what I like to call a five-minute quick-hold meditation. Select a crystal to work with and hold it in your hand. Close your eyes and take a few deep breaths. Then let your breathing go naturally. Feel the energy of the crystal you are holding and visualize the radiant colors of the crystal surrounding your whole body in a beautiful positive energy. Do this for about five minutes, and when you are finished, notice if you feel lighter, refreshed, or more peaceful than you did before.

---

[3] Debbie Hardy, *Meditation Made Easy Using Crystals: A Guide for Using Crystals during Meditation to Heal Physical, Mental, and Emotional Issues and Deepen Spiritual Connection* (Charleston, SC: CreateSpace, 2017).

Mini Meditation

This mini guided meditation will help you release all that is holding you back. You can read through it first to get an idea of how to go about it and then practice the meditation. Or you could record it into a recording device and then listen to it guide you into the meditation. Do not rush through it. Take your time instead.

Select one or more of the suggested crystals to work with during this meditation. Find a place where you will be comfortable and will not disturbed for a short period of time. It is optional, but you can add your favorite essential oils, incense, or sage at this time as well. Then sit or lie down, hold your crystals, and close your eyes.

> Take a nice deep cleansing breath in.
> Exhale all the stress and worry of the day.
> Take another nice healing, cleansing breath in.
> Exhale all the concerns on your mind.
> Take a deep healing, cleansing breath in.
> Exhale all that no longer serves you.
> Let your breathing go nice and steady and easy.
> Feel the energy from the crystal you are holding in your hand.
> Feel the crystal's energy surrounding you and protecting you in a beautiful radiant energy.
> This crystal energy will assist you in releasing what you personally need to release in order to manifest your desires.
> Now visualize in your mind being surrounded in a bubble of universal white radiant light.
> You are safe and protected in this light.
> Next, focus your attention on any tension that you may have in your body.
> It can be in your neck, forehead, jaw, back, or any other part of your body.

Start to release the tension in that area.

Feel it loosening up and visualize it dissolving.

Take a nice deep breath in, and as you exhale, release any other tension that is holding you back.

Just let it go.

Feel the tension being replaced with warmth and a sense of peace.

Let your breathing return to a nice and steady rhythm.

Now focus your attention on what is holding you back.

It could be anger, sadness, frustration, doubt, negative thoughts, a feeling of lack, or any other negative energy.

Whatever it is that is holding you back, it is time to release it.

Take a breath in, and as you exhale, exhale that specific issue that you need to release.

Just let it go with your exhaled breath, up and away, dissolving into thin air.

It does not serve you; it is time to let it go.

Tell yourself that it is OK to let it go.

If you need to forgive yourself or anyone else, you can do that now.

Tell yourself that you welcome healing and peace to occur within.

Take another nice deep breath in, and as you exhale, you will be filled with peace and calmness.

Take a few moments to continue to release all the areas that are blocking you from your desires.

Just go one by one and release them upon exhaling your breath.

Feel the negative energies dissolving and floating away from you.

When you release negative energy, you allow positive energy to enter your being.

Continue to breath nice and steady.

Begin to feel peaceful, calm energy surrounding your whole body and flowing into your heart.
Notice how light and good you feel. Notice how relaxed you feel.
Notice how completely at peace you feel.
Take a moment to just relax and be in the beautiful moment of peace.
You may remain in this space for as long as you feel the need.
When you are ready, open your eyes and return back.

This concludes the mini releasing meditation. You can do this mini meditation anytime you feel the need to release something that is holding you back.

For optimum results, you can incorporate several of these exercises at once. For example, take your journal (or paper and pen), crystals, and sage or essential oil, and go to a place outside where you can spend some quiet time. Begin by lighting your sage or place a few drops of essential oil on yourself or your crystal. Sit comfortably wherever you are, and journal your emotions and how you are feeling. Then close your eyes, take a few deep breaths, and as you exhale, feel the crystal energy begin to surround you. Then sit quietly in meditation, holding the crystal. Continue to breathe in and out quietly as you do so. Continue this for as long as you are able or as time permits. When you finish, open your eyes and spend a few quiet moments looking at the beauty that surrounds you. Listen to the sounds, and feel the warmth of the sun or the gentle breeze. When you are ready, journal how you feel afterward. Did you notice any changes in your tension level? Do you feel less stressed? Do you feel more at peace? Journal all that comes to you. Then be sure to extinguish the sage before you put it away for next time.

Negative energies can affect many things in addition to the manifestation process. If you are trying to manifest something and you are currently in a state of anger, fear, or any other negative energy, manifestation is less likely to occur. Clearing negative energies is the first part of the process to open the flow of manifestation. You want to be in alignment with peace, joy, and gratitude. Reducing the negative energy you are holding on to is the initial step in the process. Once you have accomplished this phase, you should start noticing some differences in your physical, emotional, and mental states. Some people may need to do some of these exercises a few times and others just once. Do not rush the process; I cannot stress that enough. Take the time to do these exercises so that you achieve the best possible results. Once you eliminate or reduce the negative energy consuming you, then you allow the positive energy to flow into its place. Using the suggested crystals during this phase helps to release negative energies in order to bring in a more positive vibration to your being. You can use journaling, aromatherapy, connection with nature, and meditation, along with crystal energy, to help achieve the release of negative energy. Try the various suggestions in different ways to see what works best for you, but continue to hold the crystals you decide to work with for each suggested area.

The process I typically use is to combine some journaling with sage smudging. Then I connect with nature for a bit before meditating. During these processes, I will hold or place near me certain crystals that correlate with what I am trying to achieve. Maybe you want to skip the journaling and just sit out in nature to complete a quick-hold meditation. Or maybe you would prefer to use essential oils and try a regular meditation. The choice is yours. Find what works best for you to release your current state of negative energy.

Use one or combine several of the following exercises to enhance your experience:

- In your journal, list all the things that are blocking you or holding you back and the circumstances surrounding those things (fear, anger, stress, worry, etc.).

- Add some plant-based energy for added benefit, such as sage, incense, essential oils, or aroma sprays.

- Get out in nature: go for a walk on the beach, hike in the mountains, or sit in the garden.

- Meditate for at least ten to twenty minutes daily or as often as possible.

- Practice quick-hold meditation with crystals.

- Use the mini guided meditation provided.

Finding Your Joy

I hope that you have now eliminated or at least reduced some of the negative energy that was surrounding you when you began this journey. The next part of the process is finding your joy. Finding your joy is much easier to do after eliminating negative energy. It is also an important part of the process because it raises your vibration to a positive level and allows you to be open to receive positive things. In addition, when you wish for something to manifest and you do so with a joyful heart, it is much more likely to occur than without a joyful heart. To reiterate what we discussed in the previous chapter, if you request something while being in a state of sadness, anger, or frustration, for example, it is less likely to occur. If you say something like "I really want a new job" in a state of anger because you are unhappy with your current job, then more than likely you will not get the job you are hoping for. But if you find joy in your heart, and you raise your vibration to a positive level, and then state, "I really want that new job, and I am so grateful to have the opportunity to apply for it and be considered for it," you will start to see changes and shifts in the right direction that will lead you to a new job opportunity. You may not get that specific job, but I believe you will open the flow of energy to lead you to the right job that makes you happy. It is the law of attraction: When you feel joy, you will receive joy. When you feel happy, you will receive happiness. If you feel anger and frustration, you will receive more of the same. We want to find that state of joy and hold on to it while we go through the various phases of the manifestation process. This can be a challenge for some people, but it is important to get to the point of finding your joy and holding on to it for as long as possible. The more often you are in a joyful state of being, the more positive things will radiate to you.

The suggested crystals to use during this part of the process are citrine, aventurine, emerald, carnelian, ocean jasper, or jade. Choose one or more to work with for this phase. These crystals bring joy and happiness, and they are associated with abundance as well.

Quiet Visualization

To begin this phase, select a crystal from the suggested list and hold it in your hand. Feel its beautiful energy surrounding your whole body with positive, pure radiant light.

Then close your eyes and visualize something that brings you great joy. See it in your mind's eye. It can be a person, perhaps a child or loved one, a pet, a certain food or drink, a particular place you visited, or even a special experience. Let a smile appear on your face as you think of the memory of this person, place, or thing that gives you great joy. Feel the warmth surrounding you and feel your heart expanding in joy, happiness, and love for that moment.

For example, when I try to find my joy, I think of my dogs. They greet me with such unconditional love every day when I get home that I feel their immediate love and affection, and it always brings a smile to my face regardless of what kind of day I have had. Find the joy that makes you forget any issues, problems, or challenges you may be facing and hold it in your heart. Let yourself feel that joy as if you were experiencing whatever it was that brought that joy to you.

Journal Exercise

Next, as you continue to hold your selected crystal, get your journal and write down some things that make you happy. Let the words flow and write the details of those people, places, things, or experiences that let the joy and happiness into your heart. You may find that there are many things that bring joy to your daily life; some of those things we often forget.

I AM Statements

Another good way to hold your joy is to write I AM statements on sticky notes and place them around your work space or home. I AM statements are powerful because the words you place behind I AM is what you become or what you are. Write some I AM statements on a few sticky notes and place them near your computer, mirror, coffee cup, or anywhere else where you will see them often. Every time you see the sticky note statement, say what is written on it. The more you say it, the more you begin to feel it. The more you begin to feel it, the more you begin to believe it. Place your joy crystals on or near the I AM sticky notes as a reminder to hold your crystals as you say the I AM statements.

Write such statements as the following:
- I AM filled with joy.
- I AM so very happy.
- I AM filled with radiant joy and happiness.

Get creative with it. I use I AM statements often. I place them by my mirror and desk to remind myself to say those things that help keep me on track. Especially if I am having a stressful or challenging day, I will remind myself to say the I AM statements to bring myself back to my joy and to release the negative energies from the day. You do not have to limit these to just joy statements. You can do this for anything you wish to achieve or become. The key here is to keep it positive and to say it with meaning and joy in your heart.

Finding joy in your heart raises your vibration to a more positive level and you become open to receiving positive things in your life. In addition, if you state your intention with a joyful heart, it is much more likely to occur. Take the time you need to find your joy. Remember, this process cannot be rushed. You will know when you are ready to move on to the next phase. I do want to stress how important it is to clear the negative and to find your joy before you begin the next phase.

Use one or more of the following suggestions to connect to the state of joy:

- List people, places, things, or experiences in your journal that bring you such great joy that you smile and your heart expands with happiness.

- Journal all the things that bring joy to your life.

- Write some joyful I AM statements, set them in various places, and say them often.

Expressing Gratitude

Although each phase of the manifestation process is important, gratitude is the most essential of all. If you can find complete gratitude in your heart—when you feel overwhelmed with gratitude, joy, and happiness—so many positive things will flow to you. You will open the channels to allow positive vibrations to manifest your wishes. If you practice gratitude and going to a deeper state of gratitude, then all sorts of positive things begin to shift and change. When I ask people what they are grateful for, they typically answer their families, homes, loved ones, and so on. I want you to reach such a deep state of gratitude that your heart expands and overflows with it. It is wonderful to be grateful for those typical things, but there is so much more that we should realize when we practice gratitude. Get ready to dive deep into gratitude!

When I first decided I was going to change my state of being and bring myself out of the depressed state I was in, I practiced gratitude daily, and I continue to do so to this day. I believe that it influenced my life in so many ways. By being grateful for what I had, I felt it opened the floodgates of manifestation to me within a short amount of time. I was able to see results quickly. When I do these gratitude exercises, I feel such deep gratitude that I am beyond words. The words *thank you* do not begin to express how I feel, and quite often it brings tears to my eyes because I am so grateful. I practice gratitude each morning and evening by giving thanks for each and every thing and experience I can think of. Many times I go to sleep with a smile on my face for feeling such gratitude, and I wake up feeling the same way. What an amazing feeling! That is where we want to get you—flowing with gratitude.

There is only one suggested crystal listed for this chapter: rose quartz. Rose quartz brings an abundance of love, and I believe it is the perfect choice to work with while finding gratitude. Rose quartz is such a loving stone that it is something you can wear or carry with you day and night. It will become your constant companion and reminder of your gratitude practices. If you are so inclined, carry it with you all day; you can even place it under your pillow at night. It is easy to love the energy of rose quartz, and if you do these practices often, you may want to have a few tumbles on hand.

We will be doing a gratitude exercise, and we are going to take it to a deep level. Hold your rose quartz each time you do this process. Get your journal, and I will talk you through the process of going deep with gratitude. Then you can select your own object to work with and journal your experience with and your thoughts on it. You will find there are many layers and levels to all the things we use on a daily basis, and this technique can quickly open your awareness and receptibility for manifestation.

Going Deep with Gratitude

For this example, I will use a cup of coffee. If you do not drink coffee, follow along with this example anyway, then you will have the opportunity to work on your own gratitude exercise. I just want you to get a feel for how to go deep with finding gratitude. Think about when you take that first sip of coffee in the morning. How does it make you feel? Think about the flavor and the warmth that it provides. Does it make you feel satisfied, awake, ready to start your day, and happy? How else does it make you feel? The next time you take a sip of coffee, really savor the flavor of it, really taste it, and be thankful for all that it provides you as well as for the wonderful flavor that it gives you. Next, think of how you prefer your coffee. Do you add cream, sugar, or other flavorings? Do you drink it from a mug, paper cup, or coffee cup?

As you think about your coffee, also think about all the people who are involved in creating it. Think about all the elements that grew the plants, including the water and soil. Then think about those who planted the seeds, harvested the beans, roasted and ground the beans, packed them, and shipped them to where you ultimately bought your coffee. Think about all the people who deliver them to the stores and put them on the shelves as well as the checkout clerks. Give thanks to all those involved in the various processes. Think of the vehicle that you drive to go to the store to buy your coffee and all those involved in creating your vehicle. Next, think of all the packaging the coffee goes into and who created it as well as all the equipment needed to package it. What about the other things you use in your coffee, such as sugar or sweetener? Who was involved in harvesting or creating those items and their packaging?

What if you order your ground coffee online? Think of all the people who put it on the websites and packaged it and shipped it to your door. Now we'll take this to another level. If you made that cup of coffee at home, think about those who created your coffee maker and its filters as well as the cup that you drink it from and the spoon that you stir it with. Think about the water and electricity that you use and who brought those elements into your home.

If you went to a store, such as Starbucks, and purchased a cup of coffee, consider all those involved in getting the coffee to those places, in growing the coffee, and in creating the cups that it goes in. It is truly amazing to think about all the many layers, people, and elements involved in creating one cup of coffee, all working in harmony just for you to take that first sip every morning.

Thousands upon thousands of people are involved in one way or another so that you can take that first sip of coffee each day. Take a moment to send a silent, heartfelt thank-you to each person involved. Of course you cannot know who these people are, and they will not know that you sent them thanks, but on some energetic level, they will receive the gratitude you sent. This also creates a space in your heart that becomes filled with gratitude once you start counting all the possibilities of others involved. There are so many other layers that I did not even mention that you may be able to think of too.

Once you think about all the many layers that are involved in just a simple cup of coffee, how does it make you feel that it is so convenient just to put the coffee in your coffee maker or to pick it up somewhere? Sometimes we take so many things for granted, but there are many levels and layers to each thing we have, and we have so much to be grateful for. This is how we take gratitude to the next level and open our hearts to be able to receive many great things.

Gratitude Exercise

Do this gratitude journaling exercise on your own. Find some quiet time, hold your rose quartz, and select an object that you have in front of you. Take it as deep as you can possibly think about and give thanks to all those involved in getting that object to you as they did. Write in your journal the object you chose to focus on and then all the things that come to you about the creation of that object, all the processes, the people, and anything else that comes to mind. Then journal how it makes you feel after the gratitude exercise. How do you feel after taking gratitude to such a deep level? Next, send all those involved a silent, heartfelt thank-you. Once you have done this process, notice if you feel more grateful for the object you selected. Do you feel more grateful for the people involved in creating the object? Do you feel more grateful that you are able to obtain this object?

The more you practice this gratitude exercise, the more you will see a shift in your energy. It will quickly rise to a positive level, which opens the flow of the law of attraction and manifestation. Do not be surprised if you notice yourself starting to think of all those involved with the many things you experience or have. When you reach that positive level, you will start to see changes happening and you truly can open yourself to some profound manifestation. I suggest that you practice this as often as you can to keep yourself at the optimum level of receiving.

Gratitude Altar

To continue the flow of gratitude within your daily life, you might want to create a gratitude altar. I suggest finding a space in your bedroom or other meditative space where it will not be disturbed by others or pets. Find a place where you can set it up and leave it. You will need a rose quartz point, candles, and a glass jar (such as a mason jar), a vase, or a wooden box. Add some flowers, or flower petals, and essential oils—either rose, lavender, or other flower oil—if you wish. Do not over think it. Have fun with it and let the creativity flow. Place a rose quartz point in the center space of your altar. Place a candle on either side of the point; you can add more candles if you are guided to do so. You can add other crystals or items as you feel the need. Let your intuition guide you. Place a mason jar, vase, or wood box to hold your gratitude lists for the day behind the rose point. Have a pen and some sticky notes nearby. At the end of each day, sit by your altar for five to ten minutes, light the candles, look at the beauty you have created, and give thanks for the day. Write as many things as you can think of to be grateful for that day on the sticky note, fold it, and place it in the jar, vase, or box. Silently give thanks for each item on your list and let your heart swell with gratitude. Blow out the candles when you are finished and then return the next day to do the same. You can also hold your rose quartz tumbled stone during this process.

There will be some days when it is not possible to spend time at your altar, but the more you can continue the flow of gratitude within your being, the more you will see many positive changes occur within your life. You can make the altar as simple or as intricate as you like. The more you like looking at it and spending time in that space, the more likely you will want to do the gratitude work.

Here is an example of my gratitude altar. I have a glass vase in the back and a rose point sitting on an engraved selenite round, with a candle on each side. I also have three rose quartz palm stones that form a triangle around the point. There are two small angels, one rose quartz and the other amethyst, on the sides and one small selenite heart in the front. When flowers are in bloom, I choose some from my garden and add those to my altar. I have rose oil next to my altar, along with a lighter, pen, and sticky notes.

Giving Thanks

It is important to give thanks in a simple way each morning and night. This is in addition to the gratitude altar exercise, but it is quick and simple and provides amazing results. Each morning, as soon as you wake up and before you do anything else, say, "Thank you, I am blessed" three times. Feel the gratitude as you state these words with feeling. Mean it as you say it, because if it holds no meaning for you, it will not work. You have to really feel what you are saying and let your heart expand with the beautiful, simple words, "Thank you, I am blessed." Then go about your day. At the end of the day, right before you go to bed at night, say, "Thank you, I am blessed" three times. Again, do this with heartfelt meaning and let yourself feel the words as you say them. This will allow you to go to sleep in a state of gratitude and to wake the same way. It is a simple, fast, and effective way to make a positive change in your life.

When your heart is filled with gratitude, more positive energy flows to you. This is what makes the manifestation process open and flow your wishes and desires to you. By sending silent heartfelt words of thanks to others who are involved with what you have, it sends a positive vibration to those people as well as to the universe. The universe responds in kind because it knows the grateful vibration you sent out, and it will send something amazing to you in return. When you are truly grateful, wonderful things begin to happen. It is a big shift in positive energy. Continue your gratitude journaling exercises often and when you want to manifest something to open your heart with such profound gratitude. Hold that feeling of deep gratitude for as long as you can and let your heart overflow with gratitude!

Use one or more of the following gratitude exercises:

- Select an object and go even deeper by writing everything that comes to you about the object.

Describe it and then think of all the people who created that object, how it got to the place you purchased it from, all the people involved at the place you purchased it from, the packaging, the care that was taken to get it to the store. Go as deep as you possibly can. This process fills your heart with such deep gratitude. Remember to send a silent thank-you to all those involved in creating and getting that object to you.

• Create a gratitude altar and use it daily or as often as possible.

• Say, "Thank you, I am blessed" three times each morning upon waking and each night before going to bed.

Focusing on Your Intention

The next phase is to focus clearly on what you want to manifest. It is important to be very clear about what it is that you want to manifest. If you have doubts, or you are unsure or question certain things about what you want, then the law of attraction will respond as unsure and doubtful. You get what you think. In this chapter, we will work on getting a clear picture of what it is that you want, and within the next few chapters, you will set your intentions.

For example, if you think you want a new car but you do not have all the details of the car mapped out in your mind, then you may end up getting a car that does not have everything you want. Focus clearly on all the details of the car you want: the color, style, make and model, and anything else you want in that car. Think about the interior and how it feels when you drive it. Get as specific as you can with what you want to manifest.

Have you experienced a time when you thought you wanted something but you were not completely sure that you really wanted it? I have experienced this in the past. Years ago, I was considering applying for a new position that opened up at my workplace because of the increase in salary. However, as I started thinking about the position, I was not completely sure that I wanted to start learning a whole new job and routine. Plus, I would have different hours and responsibilities. I applied for the position because of the money, but I was not totally convinced that I wanted to make such a big change. I interviewed for the position and it went very well. However, I did not get the job, and I feel it was because my complete mind and heart were not totally invested in getting that position. My hesitation shifted the energy. I still might not have gotten that specific position anyway, but something else might have come along if I had been clearer about what I wanted.

The suggested crystals to use for this phase are fluorite, clear quartz, or sodalite. These are effective for finding clarity and focus. I use fluorite every time I need to focus on something. I keep one on my work desk at all times.

Quiet Brainstorming

To begin this exercise, hold your chosen crystal and have your journal handy. Close your eyes for a moment and take three deep breaths in and out; then just let your breathing go natural, steady and easy. Clear your mind by focusing your attention on the energy the crystal is surrounding you with. Continue to keep your eyes closed for a moment as you consider what you want to manifest. Holding your crystal, brainstorm all the things you wish to manifest, and then open your eyes and write them in your journal. You do not have to get detailed yet; just write down all the things you wish to do, achieve, or obtain. Let the process flow onto the paper.

Maybe you would like your body to return to a healthy state or you'd like to lose weight. Perhaps you want a career change or just to get a job. Possibly you would like to follow your true passion and have the means to do so. Write down everything that comes to you, and take as long as you need to for this process.

When you are finished, look over your list and decide what is the most important thing on it that you wish to manifest. Write the number one next to it or circle it.

Visualization Exercise

Once you have decided what you want to manifest, you must visualize it. Visualization is picturing something in your mind with your eyes closed. Continue to hold your chosen crystal, close your eyes, and take a few deep breaths in and out. Then let your breathing go steady and natural. Next, visualize in your mind what you want to manifest. Now we will start filling in the details. See in your mind, with perfect clarity, exactly what you want. If it is an object, visualize the size, color, make, model, and anything else you can think of in detail. If you want to manifest love, visualize the perfect partner, the common interests you would like that person to have, the loving relationship between you, the person's age and looks, and whatever else it is that you want in a perfect relationship. If you want to manifest good health, then see your body as vibrant, energetic, and healthy in every way. Take a few moments to really see your request with all the details of how you would like it to manifest.

Continue with your eyes closed and begin to see it perfectly in your mind and feel it perfectly in your body, mind, and spirit. Feel it as if it has already occurred and what it would feel like if you had what it is you want right this very moment. Let yourself enjoy the sensation of what it would feel like if it were yours right now. Hold that amazing feeling within you, and allow a smile to appear on your face. Allow yourself to feel great about what you requested because what you requested is important. If it is important to you, then it is important. Open your eyes and journal how you are feeling. I hope that you are feeling amazing! That is where we want you to be, feeling amazing.

In the following chapters, I will guide you in sending your wish or prayer up to the universe for manifestation. This visualization exercise helps you clarify what it is that you want to manifest and to see it in detail. This is another important step in the process. If you are unclear or undecided about something, then you will send mixed signals to the universe and you may not receive exactly what you were hoping for. If you take the time to think through what you want as specifically as you can, and if you are clear with the details, then you have a better chance of getting exactly what you have requested. The law of attraction says that you get what you think about, so keep your thoughts clear.

Be sure to do the following exercises:

•   Brainstorm. List all the things you want to focus on manifesting now. It can be material things (car, home, etc.), a job/career, health and well-being, peace of mind, a new learning experience or direction, travel, self-improvement, or anything else you can think of.

•   Journal all that comes to you and then determine the most important thing on your list at this time.

•   Visualize your manifestation request in all its details, then visualize what it would feel like if it already occurred.

•   Journal how you felt after the exercise.

Maintaining a Positive Vibration

The next phase is to maintain a positive vibration throughout the rest of the manifestation process. It is important to reduce or release the negative energy to allow the positive energy in. By now I hope you have released some negative energy, found your joy, experienced some deep gratitude, and have focused clearly on what you want. The next important part of the process is to obtain a positive attitude or outlook. If you are in a positive mind-set when you request something to manifest, you are more likely to obtain it than if you are in a negative mind-set. If you hold negative thoughts while you request something, do you think you will receive what you want? If you think positive thoughts, then positive things will come your way. This is another component of the law of attraction. For example, if you want a new job and you think to yourself, "I want that job, but I know I won't get it because things just don't work out for me," will you get the job? More than likely not. But if you say, "I want that new job! I am positive it is meant for me and I am the right person for it!" and do so with an upbeat, positive attitude, and if you say it often, then you send positive vibrations out to the universe and you will have a better chance of getting the type of job you hope for. It may not be the specific job you're wishing for, but you will open yourself up to receiving positive things, and you may get an even better job. I have a friend who did this exercise and she received a multitude of job offers from which to choose!

Some of the suggested crystals you can use for finding positive energy and maintaining a positive attitude are clear quartz, emerald, citrine, pyrite, and sunstone. Clear quartz is the most abundant in positive energy and is highly effective, but the others will also work well for this process. Choose the one that you are drawn to most.

Affirmations

Hold your selected crystal for this phase and let's begin by saying some positive affirmations. Affirmations are the action or process of affirming something to be so.

Try the following:

- I am a positive and loving person and I allow positive things to come to me.
- I am a positive, loving person and I am deserving.
- I surround myself with positive, loving light.
- I am filled with positive energy and I extend positive energy in all that I do.
- Positive energy flows to me and through me in all that I do.

Use one of these statements or create your own and write it on a sticky note; carry it with you throughout the day. State your affirmation several times throughout the day, and when you do, feel it to be so. Feel the words resonating with you and feel yourself becoming what you say, but be sure to keep it positive!

Mini Meditation

This mini guided meditation will help you find positive energy and hold on to it. You may want to read through it before you do the exercise or have someone read it to you. You can even record it in your own voice and listen to the recording. Take your time with this; let yourself really experience the flow of positive energy. For this particular exercise, I suggest that you hold two crystals from the list, one in each hand.

Hold your selected crystals, one in each hand, and find a place where you can sit or lie down for a few minutes without being disturbed.

Leave the electronics behind for a bit.

Once you have found a place where you can be comfortable and will not be disturbed, close your eyes.

Take a deep healing, cleansing breath in, and exhale all the stress and worry of the day.

Take another deep healing, cleansing breath in, and exhale all that concerns you.

Take one more deep healing, cleansing breath in, and exhale all that no longer serves you.

Now let your breathing go natural and steady.

Focus your attention on the crystals you are holding and feel their energy.

It is a very positive energy.

This energy is surrounding your whole body.

Feel this beautiful positive, radiant energy.

Next, visualize that a beautiful universal light surrounds you.

Feel the warmth and security in this bubble of light.

This is a very protective and healing light.

Notice the color of the light that surrounds you.

You are safe in this place and you are encompassed by positive energy.

Feel the positive energy around your whole being.

Notice how it feels, how peaceful it feels, and overall how good it feels.

You are filled with positive energy, love, and light, and when you leave this space, you will take that energy with you.

Take as long as you need to enjoy the feel of the energy surrounding you.

When you are ready, take another deep breath in, exhale, and then open your eyes.

Notice how you feel physically, mentally, and emotionally.

You can use this mini meditation as often as you need to for a boost of positive energy.

It can be difficult to maintain a positive attitude all the time. The more you can do so, the more positive energy will flow to you. When you allow positive energy to flow to you, that is when manifestation occurs. If you find yourself in a negative state for any reason during this process, you can repeat the releasing of negative energy chapter or the maintaining positive energy chapter.

Try the following exercises to maintain a positive energy flow:

- Positive I AM affirmations. Write them on sticky notes and say them often throughout the day.

- Complete the mini meditation to connect to positive energy.

State Your Intention

To build on the previous work, it is now time to state your wishes, intentions, prayers, or requests for what you want to manifest. You will want to be sure you have cleared any negative blocks, found your joy and gratitude, focused clearly on what you want, and have a positive attitude prior to stating your intention and sending it to the universe. During this process, try to hold on to the joy, gratitude, and positive energy that you have already obtained.

In this chapter, we will be working on writing and then stating your intentions. Then you will work on visualization. I have also included a guided meditation to talk you through the complete process. Even though it is a bit repetitive, I suggest that you do all the exercises in this chapter to get the full effect. Make sure to schedule enough time to accomplish the writing, stating, visualizing, and meditating in one sitting. Again, do not rush the process. It is best that you feel each component as you experience it. By setting intentions during meditation, you are doing so at a deep state of peace, trust, and calmness that can make an overall difference in receiving what you wish for. Take the time to go through the meditation as well.

Some of the crystals I suggest you work with during this phase are green aventurine, carnelian, emerald, jade, pyrite, tiger eye, clear quartz, or citrine. I have used each of them for manifestation, and they all provide a slightly different added benefit, so you can use more than one during this phase if you choose to do so. Although they are all good for manifestation, I will give you a bit more information on each of them so that you can determine which you want to work with.

- Green aventurine is good for bringing happiness and positive energy.
- Carnelian is good for bringing energetic stimulation and creativity.
- Emerald is good for inspiration and patience.
- Jade is good for wisdom.
- Pyrite is good for bringing luck, confidence, abundance, and protection.
- Tiger eye is helpful for good fortune and protection.
- Clear quartz is good for positive energy and amplifying the energy of the other crystals you choose.
- Citrine helps you maintain a joyful attitude. You can use heat-treated citrine (amethyst heated to citrine) or natural citrine. Natural citrine is a bit more expensive and sometimes harder to find. I have used both for my personal manifestation practices and I have had success with each.

As you look over this list, you might feel overwhelmed as you try to decide which crystals to work with during this phase of the process. Use and trust your intuition to help you choose the ones that will be in alignment with what you want.

I have worked with all these crystals and have had great results in doing so, but I also want to mention the power trio: citrine, green aventurine, and pyrite. These three crystals are an amazing combination of energy associated with manifestation and abundance. The other contributing factors of joy, confidence, and helping you stay heart centered are important during the manifestation process. If you can, try adding the power trio during the setting intentions phase or grid work (discussed in a following chapter).

Next, you will want to hold your selected crystals during this process, gather your journal, and write out your intention (wish, prayer, request). Be as clear as you can. If you need to return to the journal exercise of brainstorming to find the intention you marked as number one, you can do so.

Write and Speak Your Intention

Begin with the fragment "I want to manifest..." and then fill in the remainder of the sentence. For example, if you want a new job, write something like "I want to manifest the perfect new job that will pay a grand salary and have excellent benefits, with a positive work environment and shared vision." Write it as positively as possible. If you want a new car, state the make, model, color, and any other important details you want to include. Hold your selected crystals, take a moment to write your intention statement, and when you are satisfied with it, say it out loud with a joyful and happy heart. Remember, if you state something with no enthusiasm, then you will be less likely to obtain what you ask for, but if you state it with a positive, joyful, and happy attitude, the universe responds in kind and the law of attraction responds to the positive vibrations you have set forth. Take your time during this exercise. It is not something you want to rush. It is important to remember to be clear, to state your intention with a joyful, happy heart, and to be grateful!

Visualize Your Intention

Continue to hold your selected crystals for the visualization exercise. Once you have written and stated your intention, close your eyes and visualize your intention in your mind. See your request floating up to the universe like an envelope drifting up to the heavens, its open hands receiving your letter. Next, take a moment to see it clearly as it manifests. See it as if you already have what you ask for and it is perfect. Think about how it would feel if you had what you requested right now. Would you be excited, thrilled, feel like celebrating? Hold that feeling as you continue to visualize your manifestation request happening. Then open your eyes and jot down in your journal how you feel right after this process.

Meditation for Manifestation

You can read through this meditation first and then try it on your own, or you could have someone read it to you. You can even record this into a recording device and then listen to it, with your own voice prompting you through the journey.

Select your crystals and find a quiet place to sit or lie down for a period of time during which you will not be disturbed. Once you find that place, hold your crystals in each hand or place them around your body, and I will lead you through a journey to open up manifestation.

> When you are ready, close your eyes.
> Let's begin by taking a deep healing, cleansing breath in.
> Exhale all the stress or tension of the day.
> Inhale another deep healing, cleansing breath in.
> Exhale all the worries or concerns you are holding on to.

Take one more deep healing, cleansing breath in, and exhale all that no longer serves you.

Now let your breathing go easy and steady.

Visualize in your mind a beautiful, radiant universal light surrounding your body.

This is a protective, healing light and you are safe in this place.

Now visualize any area of your body that might have negative energy or tension.

Take a moment or two to release that negative energy or tension.

Take a breath in, and as you exhale, feel the tension and negative energy dissolving and floating away from your body.

You will begin to feel more relaxed and peaceful.

Now take one more nice deep breath in, and as you exhale, feel a state of peace and calmness surround you.

Next, visualize in your mind a person, place, thing, or experience that brings you great joy.

It can be a child, a pet, a place you love to visit, or a certain experience that filled you with joy.

Revisit that person, place, thing, or experience now. Feel that joy returning to you, feel your heart expanding with joy, and allow yourself to smile as you think about it.

Hold that joy as long as you can.

Now think of something you are truly grateful for. Something that expands your heart in such gratitude that there are not enough words to express how grateful you are for it.

Think about what it is that brings you to such a deep state of gratitude. Be aware of your gratitude and continue holding your gratitude and joy in your heart.

Notice how wonderful it feels to be in such a deep state of gratitude and joy.

You have lifted your vibration to allow wonderful things to happen for you.

As you continue to hold the joy and gratitude in your heart, clearly think about what you want to manifest. Get a clear picture of it in your mind and take a moment to visualize all the details.

See the details of how it will be exactly so that it is perfect for you.

Continue to hold that joy and gratitude in your heart.

Now send your request to the universe.

State in your mind, "I request..." and complete the rest of the sentence with your wish.

Take a moment to do that now.

See your request floating up to the universe like a letter floating up to the heavens.

Visualize your wish coming true.

See it happening and think about how it would feel for it to occur.

You have planted the seed today.

You have sent your request, and the universe has received it.

Hold a positive attitude that things will work out exactly as you requested—or even better.

Take a moment to thank the universe for hearing, receiving, and responding to your request.

Thank you, thank you, thank you.

Take a breath in, and as you exhale, just let it go for the universe to handle.

Remember to continue to hold joy and gratitude in your heart and take another moment to truly give a heartfelt thank-you to the universe for helping you receive what you wished for.

When you are ready, open your eyes.

Be sure that you are in a positive state of mind and that you feel joyful when you state your intention. It does make a difference. Take the time to experience the meditation to amplify the intention-setting process.

Exercises for this phase include the following:

- Write out your intention as clearly as possible, then say it out loud in a joyful, upbeat frame of mind.
- Visualize your intention being sent to the heavens and then being received by the universe.
- Visualize and think about how it would feel if your wish has already come true. How would that feel? Journal what comes to you.
- Complete the meditation for manifestation.

Sending Blessings

Have you ever heard that a blessing sent is a blessing received? If you send blessings (well wishes) to another person, then you receive blessings in return, which continues the positive cycle of giving and receiving. This is an important component of the process. In addition, it feels amazing to send blessings to others; it raises the positive vibration tremendously quickly. The universe plays a huge role in helping us get what we want, but we also have to depend on other humans. The universe shifts things in order for your manifestation request to occur, and one common occurrence is that the universe sends others who can help us along the way. Think about everything you have ever wanted. Were humans involved in each of those requests in some way? We need to be grateful for their assistance and send them blessings. This not only helps them with whatever they are going through but also helps us!

For this exercise, hold your rose quartz. Rose quartz is such a lovely frequency of the heart, and if you send heartfelt blessings, it will connect beautifully. You are likely wondering who you will be sending blessings to. I will get to that in just a moment. If you send a blessing, how you will you receive one in return? You send blessings to those who are unaware that you are doing so, and because they do not know it, they do not respond in kind, but the universe responds by sending you blessings.

Who will you send blessings to? Hold your rose quartz and get your journal. Make a list of all the types of occupations that may influence your manifestation request. For example, if you want to manifest a trip, list all the services that you would use before, during, and after your trip. List such occupations as travel agents, taxi drivers, airport clerks, pilots, ship captains, hotel personnel, waitresses, cooks/chefs, and whatever else comes to mind. Once you have your list, send a silent blessing to all those who hold such occupations. You could say something like this: "From the depths of my heart, I send blessings to all who hold such occupations as [SAY YOUR LIST] and that the right people will come to me to help me with my wishes." When you are in the right alignment, things tend to fall into place easily. Part of this is the right people showing up at the right time. The universe sends us who we need in order to obtain what we want.

Years ago when I opened my crystal shop, I had put out to the universe that I wanted a place to lease where I could sell crystals, facilitate workshops, and hold healing appointments. I requested that the best possible outcome occur. It was quite a process of finding and leasing a space, and going through the licensing, inspections, and all the city paperwork involved, but I kept sending blessings and gratitude along the way. I had never done a start-up business before and it seemed daunting, but once I became grateful to all those involved, I noticed a shift of energy. As things started happening, everything fell into place rapidly. I had my business up and running within two weeks, and that included getting all the city requirements accomplished, remodeling the space to make it inviting, and stocking it. It was an amazing whirlwind experience, but once everything began happening, I knew that the universe was sending people to assist me as well as making it easy for me to find what I needed when I needed it.

Once things begin shifting and you start to see things unfolding, then you can get more specific with your blessings. Be sure to continue to do this throughout the process of your manifestation waiting phase. For each person who assists with your manifestation request, send them a silent blessing but also give them heartfelt thanks for their assistance. It's simple and it goes a long way.

Exercises for this phase include the following:

- Make a list of all possible occupations that could assist with what you are requesting to manifest.

- Hold your rose quartz and send a silent blessing to all those who hold such occupations.

- When things begin to shift and occur, continue to send silent blessings to all those who assist you in some way and give them heartfelt thanks for their assistance.

Using an Abundance Grid

Crystal grids provide an amazing energy when set with positive intentions for manifestation. A crystal grid is the combination of crystal energy, intentions, and the geometric formation that creates such a powerful energy source to help with your manifestation process. In Hibiscus Moon's book, *Crystal Grids: How and Why They Work,* she describes a crystal grid as "a geometric pattern of energetically aligned stones charged by intention set in a sacred space for the purpose of manifesting a particular objective."[4] When you are in the right alignment (reducing the negative and allowing the positive) with the use of crystal energy, amazing things can begin to occur.

You should be in alignment at this point, so this would be a good time to create a crystal grid of your own. Let's choose abundance as an example of a generalized grid to create. This is not required, but I suggest that you give it a try. Kick up the manifestation vibration a notch and create an abundance grid yourself. You should do this shortly after you complete the previous chapters so that you are still holding the manifestation, intention-setting vibration. It does not have to be on the same day (unless you want it to be) but within the next few days. You will want to be in the positive energy state while you do this process, so have fun with it!

---

[4] Hibiscus Moon, *Crystal Grids: How and Why They Work: A Science-Based, Yet Practical Guide* (Charleston, SC: CreateSpace, 2011), 17.

Some things that I have received after I set up my grid are an increase in pay, unexpected money, discounts, free items, and gifts, among others. These things have been continuously growing and expanding since I set the grid in place. Pay attention to the changes that begin to occur after you set up your abundance grid.

When I constructed my first grid, I was still the only one who was working, so our income was limited and we had been struggling financially for several years. I selected my crystals, created my grid, and set the intention that all that is positive and pure come to us and abundance for all who live here with me. Soon after I dedicated the grid with that intention, things started to change. I got an unexpected salary increase at work, my husband got a job, and shortly thereafter he got an increase in salary. We both got bonuses soon after that! We noticed several changes continually, and we brought ourselves out of financial crisis. I still have my grid in place. I have altered it some from time to time, but it still continues to flow positive energy to us. This did not all happen overnight. Some things took a bit of time, but it has been an ongoing functional energy source since!

My grid consists of a polished natural citrine point in the center, and the tumbled stones placed in an infinity pattern are citrine (heat treated and natural for joy and abundance), emerald (for abundance), aventurine (for abundance), carnelian (for constant energy), garnet (to eliminate a sense of lack), and citrine chips. In the center of the infinity loops, I have pyrite (for abundance), a Chinese coin, and a jade coin.

Create Your Own Abundance Grid

Here is what you will need to create your own abundance grid.

- Your intention written on a sticky note or a small piece of paper that states, "I dedicate this grid to all that is positive and pure. I dedicate this grid to bring abundance and prosperity to myself and to all those who hold this space. So it is, it is so." You can change this statement to make it more personal, or you can use this one.

- Choose your crystals from any category on the crystal list. Use your intuition to help you decide.

- You will need a small clear quartz or selenite wand.

- Find a place to set the grid where it will not be disturbed by family, friends, or pets.

- Print a grid template of the circle or infinity pattern, or any other pattern that stands out to you. You can find many on Pinterest.

First decide what your abundance intention will be. I have provided what I say, but you can change it to make it more personal and to suit your own abundance needs. Be sure to keep it positive and ensure that what you will be saying resonates with you personally. You will want to write it on a sticky note because you will need it when you dedicate the grid. As mentioned earlier, my preference is: "I dedicate this grid to all that is positive and pure. I dedicate this grid to bring abundance and prosperity to myself and to all those who hold this space. So it is, it is so." I chose to include my immediate family members (those who hold this space, meaning all those who live here) because I want abundance for them as well. I think it made a difference to include my family members in my intentions, even if they were not aware of it. I feel that the energy and positive intentions helped all those who live in this space.

Next, you will need to decide what crystals to use in your grid. Some of the crystals I suggest you work with are green aventurine, carnelian, emerald, jade, pyrite, tiger eye, clear quartz, or citrine. Again, I cannot stress enough that you use your intuition to select your crystals.

For most of the exercises, I have suggested that you use tumbled stones. These are good for a grid as well, but you will have to decide if you want to use a tumbled stone or a point for the center of your grid. I have a citrine polished point in the center of my grid at the moment, but when I started, I used a small polished clear quartz point, which is more easily obtained and less expensive. You may find yourself changing and fine-tuning it as you go. You will also need a small two- to three-inch clear quartz or selenite wand to direct the grid energy. You will want to cleanse your crystals before you place them in the grid so that their energy is stable and ready to go. I suggest that you have a separate set of crystals for the grid so that you can continue using your other crystals for the manifestation phases.

The next step to creating a grid is to decide where you will put it. As with your gratitude altar, you will want to place this in a space that will not be disturbed by other family members, friends, or pets. Use your intuition when selecting where you will place the grid.

I suggest using either a circle or an infinity pattern because both are never-ending. They are both continuous cycles and will allow your abundance to continue to flow to you. You can find several crystal grid templates on Pinterest, so just print one out and use it as a guideline. You can set the crystals directly on the printout for an idea of where to place them and then remove the paper template and leave the crystals in place. There are many other grid patterns available, so if you see something else you would like to use instead, please do so. You may wonder how to go about placing your crystals on the pattern. As you can see from my example, I have two sets of tumbled stones placed on my infinity pattern. I began placing one crystal from one set and then the next and so on, and then I repeated the process on the other side of the infinity pattern, so it is a symmetrical image of itself. However, I know several others who have created crystal abundance grids with just the use of their intentions and several different crystals in no particular pattern, and they have had great success as well. If you prefer organized and symmetrical, then do that, or place the crystals based on your intuition.

Once you have the space, the crystals, and your intention, then you can begin to construct your grid. You will set your template down to get the pattern of how to place your crystals. Then you will place your crystals along the grid pattern, with a crystal in the center. Play around with it and get a feel for the energy. You may need to make some adjustments along the way.

Once you get the stones in place, remove the template if you wish to do so, and hold your sticky note with your intention so that you remember what to say. You can also place another sticky note with your intention written on it underneath the center stone if you would like to do so. Take your wand and go from stone to stone in a clockwise direction (positive energy flows clockwise) and connect the dots, so to speak. You are getting the flow of energy from crystal to crystal. As you do this, you will want to state your intention. Once you have created the energy flow and stated your intention, close your eyes for a moment and feel the energy of the crystals in the space. Visualize the flow of energy from crystal to crystal and then visualize abundance flowing to you.

You will want to spend a moment every so often looking at your grid, giving thanks for the things you have received, and appreciating its energy. If you feel the need to make adjustments to the grid, you will want to rededicate it with the energy flow and your spoken intention.

Crystal grids can be amazing helpers for the manifestation process. At this point, you should be in alignment with positive energy, so if you are inspired, try creating your own crystal abundance grid. It can be simple or intricate, but either way, have fun with it. You can create specific grids for specific intentions by using crystals that hold the energy that aligns with what you are trying to achieve. You will have to do some research on which crystals will work with your specific intention and then go from there.

Exercises for this phase include the following:
- Create your own abundance crystal grid and see what changes occur in your life.

What Happens Next?

Next is the waiting phase. This is something that none of us like to do, right? We are by nature impatient beings. I have had some wishes come true right away, whereas others took time, such as weeks or months, to receive. It is important to maintain a positive energy state during this phase, so if you need to repeat that process, do so as much as necessary. During the waiting phase, you will need to focus on being open and allowing yourself to receive what you asked for, trusting and believing it will occur, watching for signs and indications that it is happening, giving it time, and having patience for everything to happen as it should.

Open and Allowing

It is important to be open to receiving what you have asked for. You have given it to the universe to handle, so let the universe handle it. Do not concern yourself with the how, just allow things to happen and unfold. If you remain in the positive vibration, it is much easier to be open to receiving what you asked for. If you slip back into the negative vibration, you will want to pull yourself out of that state in order to release any blocks you may have put up. When you are in the state of being open and allowing to receive, I have found quite often that the universe will provide you with what you wished for or something even better.

My little dog Max passed away several years ago, and I wanted another small dog. I decided to focus on finding another little dog to be my best friend and companion, so I put an intention out, requesting the universe to help me find that perfect dog. I was specific about size, age, gender, and breed. During the waiting phase, I looked online at various rescue and pet adoption agencies. I had to exercise my patience because I wanted a dog now, but I had to allow the universe to find the right match for me. So I waited. I applied for several dogs that fit the criteria I was looking for during this time, which is a tedious process. They ask you to fill out an application, and if that is approved, they conduct a home visit to see if it is a suitable environment and meets their standards. I figured I would have no issue because my home is secure and loving, so what more could they want? However, I ran into something I never thought would happen. I was denied by several agencies, and many others never even responded to my application. I had to continually remind myself that the universe would send me the right dog when it was time. I had to keep my positive vibration up and continue to believe that everything would work out. I had to be open to receiving the perfect dog for me. I was confused by the situation, but I kept on. I also continued to receive signs and indications that the right dog would come, but it was just not time yet. One day I found another dog, and I applied for it. I filled out the application with no expectation of hearing back, but within minutes, I got a response saying I was approved. Then they sent a message to schedule a time to meet. I was thrilled and elated. I knew at that moment, even before I met the dog, that this was the one! I met this sweet little mixed breed and fell in love immediately. She was the one. I renamed her Emma and she bonded with me immediately too. She was the perfect fit for me, my home, and my family. This occurred three months after I had started the process, so you see, you must be open and allowing to receive what you had asked for or better. You have to trust and believe that it will work out, you have to pay attention to the signs and indications that it is moving along, and you have to give it the proper time to manifest. I could not have asked for a better fit as far as personality and companionship from a dog. It was better than I had hoped for; I just had to wait for it.

Open and Allowing Exercise

First, select a crystal from the suggested list. For this process, I recommend either labradorite or prenite. Labradorite is a bit more common, but either crystal will do just fine.

Find some quiet time, close your eyes, and take a few deep breaths in and out. Then let your breathing go natural and steady. Keep your eyes closed and visualize your beautiful wish floating to you from the universe. See yourself receiving it with open arms and embracing what you asked for. Thank the universe for the beautiful gift you have received and then open your eyes. Continue to allow things to unfold and happen. Continue to hold and carry your selected crystals during this phase of the process.

Trust and Believe

After you have set your intentions, it is time to trust and believe that everything will work out as you requested it to. Trusting that things will turn out as you hoped is one of the harder components of this process. Our ego and mind get in the way and try to tell us that things will not happen or that we are just wasting our time. Do not fall into the traps of the ego or the mind when that happens. That will just drag you back down to the negative vibration. You have worked so hard to get to this point, so keep the energy positive. Trust that things are happening, even though you may not see it right away. You planted the seed, so give it a bit of time to grow and trust that it is truly growing. Believe that the universe has heard and received your wish and is now working to manifest what you requested. This can be hard for some people, so be sure to hold your selected crystal during this phase as much as you need to. Have you heard the statement "Let go and let God"? In essence, this is what we are doing now. It is time to let go—to let the universe handle it and to trust that all will be OK. When you let go of control and allow the universe to step in and handle matters, amazing things begin to happen. Do not worry about the hows: how it will work, how it will be resolved, how it will happen. The universe will handle the details and take care of things if you allow it to and trust that it will happen.

There was a period of time when I had to take care of my mother's affairs, and one particular issue she had was with a government agency. My mother was unable to handle the problem, so I had to take care of it. It was a cycle of nonstop madness, and I was getting nowhere trying to resolve the matter. There is no fighting government agencies because they are so rigid with their rules and requirements. I became frustrated because nothing was getting resolved. I was trying to control the outcome, and because of that, I was defeated. Finally it clicked to ask for universal help, and I decided to set clear intentions of what I wanted to happen. I stated my positive intention out loud, and I let it go. I trusted and believed that it would all be resolved. Two weeks later, we received a letter in the mail—it was all settled!

Trust and Believe Exercise

If you are struggling with trusting and believing that your request was heard, received, and will manifest, hold your selected crystal and visualize the perfect outcome for your request. For this exercise, I suggest you choose from amethyst, clear quartz, labradorite, or sodalite.

Hold your selected crystal , close your eyes, take a few deep breaths, and in your mind visualize everything happening perfectly, effortlessly, and beautifully for your specific request. Tell yourself that it is OK to trust the process, to trust that everything will occur, and that what you wished for or something even better than you could ever imagine will come to be. Tell yourself that you believe that things are moving forward and that you will manifest results. Allow yourself to give up control and let the higher power (the universe) handle your request. Take another deep breath and open your eyes. Do this exercise as much as you need to during the waiting phase.

Signs and Indications

During this phase, you will also want to start watching for signs and indications that things are moving in the right direction. Really be aware of and open to the indications that come your way. Some indications will be straightforward while others will be more subtle. Some types of indicators can be aha moments, when something just makes sense, or they can be unusual situations that stand out to you. Maybe you will experience an extraordinary occurrence or a moment of epiphany. Watch for certain repetitive indications, such as recurring numbers or things that you hear or see more than once in a short time frame. You might get a more straightforward sign, such as a phone call, email, or letter out of the blue, that pertains to what you wanted. Really pay attention to your surroundings and to the things that happen throughout your days because you may be led in a direction that will take you where you ultimately want to go. You also may receive clear signs of paths to avoid, so consider those as well. When you experience an unusual event or occurrence, think about it and try to determine if it is related to what you asked for. When you see or experience something that may be a sign or indication, jot it down in your journal so that you can keep track of all that is happening. It can be like a puzzle at times, and you have to put the pieces together. Pay attention to the signs and indications that come to you. Even if you do not think they are related or if you do not understand them, they may make sense down the line. Continue to hold your crystals to continue to develop your awareness of the signs and indications that are presented to you.

Signs and Indications Exercise

Some crystals you can use to help you be more aware are clear quartz, selenite, sodalite, and labradorite.

Here is an exercise you can try to increase your awareness. When you increase your awareness, it becomes easier to see the signs and indications that are surrounding you. I suggest that you find a quiet place outdoors, where you can spend fifteen to twenty minutes. Bring your chosen crystal, along with your journal and a pen. I also like to light sage during this time, so if you have sage or incense, bring that too. Sit in a quiet place and light the sage if you plan to use it. Hold your crystal in your hands and close your eyes. Take a few deep breaths in and out, then let your breathing go steady and easy. With your eyes closed, listen to all the sounds that surround you. Listen to the rustling of the leaves, the singing of the birds, or whatever else you hear. Pay attention to each sound in detail. When you feel ready, open your eyes and write in your journal everything you heard. Let the words flow.

Next, look around you. Notice the leaves dancing in the breeze, the butterflies floating by. Notice all of nature in its beautiful symphony. Then write down all the things you visually noticed as well as how you feel during this time. Your journal entry could be something like this:

> I hear the breeze rustling the leaves of the tree in the center of my yard. I hear birds in the distance, talking to each other about what they will have for dinner. I

not only hear the breeze but also feel it. It is the slight wind dancing in the air, telling us that it is time to celebrate what is. I also hear the wind chimes chiming as they enter the celebration. I hear a bumblebee buzz by and a creak in the fence where a large tree in the neighbor's yard rubs against it. I see the dancing of the leaves and branches. They are all in harmony with one another. A hummingbird flew by and stopped at my almond tree, hoping to find a sweet treat. Other birds fly above during this beautiful summer evening. A lizard scurries along the brick wall at the back of the yard, and my dog runs up to see it. The air is warm, and the breeze is a beautiful, comforting contrast. The colors of the trees in the evening sun are a rich deep green. I continue to observe, and I hear and see the rustling of palm fronds from the tall palm tree across the street. There is so much energy, there is so much beauty, there is so much life, and it all seems to be in harmony with one another. I am grateful to be in this space, at this time, to be part of this experience.

Do this exercise as often as you can to expand your awareness. This not only increases awareness but also brings inspiration. When you are inspired, you open yourself up to positive energy to flow to you, which is an added benefit.

Time and Patience

It is important to give time for your manifestation request to occur. As I mentioned earlier, you planted the seeds and now you need to give them time to grow. But as you wait, be open to receiving what you asked for and watching for signs and indications that things are moving along.

There are many timeline possibilities, and I have seen wishes granted within a day or days, weeks, months, and even years.

A lot depends on what you've asked for and how you asked for it. I have had requests manifest within a few weeks to months, and it was all dependent on what I wanted. Some things I requested simply took more time.

It was during October of 2016 when I finally decided I wanted to focus on my career as a full-time crystal healer. I was working full-time as an administrative assistant in our local school district, and my shop and healing center was open part time during the evenings and weekends. I had finally made a firm decision that I wanted to run the shop/center full time, so I put it out to the universe that this is was my wish. Shortly thereafter, I started noticing shifts and changes that prompted me to move forward with my goal. I became more open with my healing work with my friends, family, and coworkers. I began feeling comfortable talking to others about my plan and expressing what I hoped to do by becoming a full-time crystal healer. The work environment I was in changed as well—as if it was prompting me to leave—and this was the perfect time to exit. My family life also changed dramatically within that time frame. My mother was in a car accident, so I was no longer able to be at a full-time day job because I was attending to her needs on a daily basis. I felt I was being prompted to seek another direction from a force greater than I can describe. The following May, I gave my notice at my day job. I was giving up a well-paying, steady, and secure position within the district. Was I uncertain? Yes, but deep down inside, I felt that everything was going to be all right, and I felt an overwhelming sense of peace come over me. I was still attending to my mother's needs, but I was also being led into a new direction. I had to close my shop because the lease was up, and with everything that was happening, I did not have time to search for a different location and I did not want to remain in that location. I kept trusting. At that point, I was out of work and I had no shop, but I still felt the force of the universe guiding me. I was trusting, which is huge in this process. I was trusting where I was going and that it would all work out. I decided to focus my attention on online crystal sales because I had quite an inventory left from my shop. I was already used to doing live streams, so I decided to offer meditations and spiritual talks online because I no longer had my shop space to do those things in person. At that moment, my online presence started growing and growing. It happened quickly and organically. I did not understand how it all happened, but at the time, I was still trusting and following where I was guided. The universe handed me what I wanted but in a better way than I could have imagined. Because my mother's care has been ongoing, now I see it clearly. If I had kept my shop open, I would still be working a full-time job, in essence. I would have had to keep regular shop hours, which would have been impossible with my mother's care involved. I was given the gift of freedom from the universe. Because I was guided to focus my services completely online, I could still work around my mother's needs easily. I became a full-time crystal healer, seller, author, and teacher, and that is exactly what I wanted, but I am able to work the hours that are best for me because I do it from home. It was an even better outcome than what I had originally hoped for. For all this to happen as it did, I had to allow myself to be open to receive and I had to continue to trust on an ongoing basis that everything would work out. I had to pay attention to all the signs and indications that things were moving forward, and I had to be patient because it took about eight months to get to the turning point of quitting my day job and becoming a full-time crystal healer. It was all worth it, as I got what I wanted and then some. Sometimes the universe does that; it provides what we want *or* something even better than we could have imagined. Even though the waiting phase can be difficult, give yourself the time to experience all the components that are within that phase.

Wishes can take time to occur. Do not give up hope! This can be a stressful time, so do not allow stress to bring you down.

Use the following exercise to dissolve the stress you may experience associated with the waiting period. Keep the crystal with you during this period as well, to keep your vibration up. I have had clients and friends go through this process several times, and I have had some report back to me that their wishes manifested within a day, others within months, and others within years. It all depends on what you are asking for, how you ask for it, and how you respond to things that happen after you ask. The added benefit of crystal energy enhances the vibration of the intention set and helps all the various phases that you go through during the manifestation process.

Time and Patience Exercise

Some of the crystals I suggest you work with to help you be patient during the waiting phase are lepidolite, amethyst, moonstone, selenite, or angelite. These crystals help bring a sense of calmness and peace in order to reduce any sense of impatience or anxiety.

Select a crystal and find a quiet place to sit for about ten minutes. If you like to use sage or incense, it would be a good time to add that as well. Light your sage (or incense), hold your crystal, get comfortable, and close your eyes. Take a few deep breaths in and out and then let yourself breathe naturally. Focus on any tension you may be feeling and visualize the tension drifting up to the heavens and dissolving completely. Feel the peace that surrounds you. Feel the love that surrounds you. Visualize a divine brilliant light that surrounds you in a bubble of calmness. You are safe in this place. Let yourself become at peace in this space. Breathe nice and steady, and enjoy this peaceful, beautiful feeling that is holding you, surrounding you, and becoming within you. Let yourself feel good in this space. Let yourself release any stress you may be experiencing as you wait for your request to occur. Tell yourself that your wish will manifest at the perfect time and everything will work out beautifully. Tell yourself that you will continue to trust and believe and that you will give the universe time to manifest your desires. You are safe, you are at peace, and you are calm. When you are ready, open your eyes and notice if you feel more at peace.

You can do this exercise as much as you need to in order to reconnect to a peaceful state. When you are in a peaceful state, there is no room for stress. When you are in a peaceful state, you allow things to occur as they should, and you find an inner knowingness that everything will work out as it should, including what you asked for.

Exercises to help with the waiting phase include the following:

- Open and allow. Take some quiet time to visualize yourself with your arms open, receiving your wishes as they come true.

- Trust and believe. Take some quiet time to allow yourself to trust and believe.

- Signs and indications. Spend fifteen to twenty minutes outdoors and listen to what you hear, look at what you see, and journal all that comes to you.

- Time and patience. Release any stress from waiting and give your request time to occur.

What If You Do Not Experience Results?

I want to take a moment to address what it means if you do not see results. It comes down to being aligned and in balance. You need to release the negative to allow the positive to flow in. If you do not feel balanced, then I suggest you go through each chapter again. There are some things to consider if you have not manifested your wish, so take a few moments to honestly answer the following questions:

- Did you give the request ample time to manifest? Some can find it difficult to be patient during this process.
- Are you trying to rush it or control it? Let things happen and unfold organically.
- Was it a big request or a small request? This can be a factor in the timeline.
- Did you release the negative energy prior to stating the wish? If you are still experiencing some negative energy in any way, you may want to revisit the releasing chapter until you feel that the negative energy is dissolved.
- Did you follow through and find joy and gratitude prior to stating the wish? It truly makes a difference how you emotionally state your wish. Continue to work on the gratitude exercises daily.
- Do you believe deep down that it will occur? If you do not believe, you can block yourself from receiving your wish.

- Was your request clear, or did you hesitate? If you hesitated or were not clear, that sends mixed signals to the universe. It may not know exactly what you want, and you may get something different from what you expected, so be very clear.

- Have you been able to hold a positive attitude throughout the process? It is so important to hold the positive energy each day. It takes practice, but it does become easier in time.

- Have you noticed any signs or indications at all? If you feel that you have not, you should release the negative energy and focus on releasing blocks, so repeat the releasing negative energy chapter.

- Were you using the suggested crystals throughout each phase? If you were not, try including crystal energy. It can add a boost of energy for each phase of the process. If you were, try a few different crystals from the list and see if that helps in certain areas. For the most part, the properties associated with crystals help many in the same way, but we are all different, so maybe the crystals you selected are not right at this time. Try some others mentioned in the chapters you repeat.

Take some time to think about what area may have been the blocking point for the manifestation to occur. I suggest that you go back and repeat any or all of the phases as needed. If you followed each phase, as well as the exercise within each phase, you should begin to notice some overall positive changes in your life.

Final Thoughts

I truly believe that the powerful combination of the law of attraction, with the use of crystal energy and setting intentions while in a positive state of being, helps the manifestation process work incredibly well. The more you go through the manifestation process as I have outlined in this book, the more it becomes easier to follow and do. Before you know it, the process becomes quicker. When you are in the right alignment to manifest your dreams, life can be amazing. There are so many new opportunities, doors that open, and things that occur on a continual basis if you constantly keep yourself in correct alignment. It does take effort and time to continually keep yourself out of the negative and in the positive. It is a process in itself, but when you are able to do it, you allow amazing things to flow to you and occur for you. Continue this practice as much as possible until you feel that you are in the right alignment more so than not.

Each part of this process is important to follow, so be sure to reduce the negative to allow the positive to flow in. Focus on finding joy and practice the gratitude exercises daily. That in itself allows for amazing things to happen rapidly. Always make sure that your intentions are clear because hesitating in any way sends mixed, confused signals to the universe. The more you do this, the more easily it will start to fall into place.

Take some time to think about your short- and long-term goals and focus on those things as if money were not an object. You have the abundance grid, which is truly amazing energy. However, for the rest of your manifestations, try to focus on what you want to do, achieve, or obtain and be clear about those intentions. Do not forget that you must trust and believe and let it go. Let the higher powers handle everything, and be open to following the signs that lead to your intention. Be open to receiving the signs and indications that are presented to you because that helps you determine what steps to take. When you find what step to take, that's when things fall into place easily and things start happening.

Also remember that things take time to occur. Some requests can happen overnight and some can take a year or more. It all depends on what you are asking for, how you asked for it, what state or frame of mind you were in at the time, how clearly you stated your intentions, and if you were able to allow signs and indications to direct your guidance.

Many of my community members have messaged me after following this process and have told me it made a big difference in their manifestation practices. I personally have had tremendous ongoing success; it continues to amplify and grow and to become something even greater than before. I hope that you find monumental success with this process and that all your wishes and dreams come true. May you be filled with abundant blessings.

Quick Reference Guide

Releasing Negative Energy

- When you begin the manifestation process, you want to reduce or eliminate negative energy so that you can allow positive energy to flow to you.

- Use the following exercises to reduce negative energy: journaling, using plant-based energy, connecting to nature, and meditating.

- Hold one or more of the following crystals during this phase: red jasper, garnet, ruby, petrified wood, black tourmaline, obsidian, smoky quartz, shungite, or hematite.

Finding Your Joy

- After you have cleared any negative energy you may be holding on to, it is important to find your joy. You will want to be in a joyful state when you set your intention because it will be more likely to occur.

- Use the following exercises to find your joy: quiet visualization, journaling, and I AM statements.

- Hold one or more of the following crystals during this phase: citrine, green aventurine, emerald, jade, or ocean jasper.

Expressing Gratitude

- Finding a deep state of gratitude can create a positive shift to allow positive energy to flow to you.

- Use the following exercises to find gratitude: gratitude exercise, create a gratitude altar, and give thanks.

- Hold a rose quartz during this phase.

Focusing on Your Intention

- Be very clear about what you want to manifest. If you have a clear focus, you are more likely to obtain what you want.

- Use the following exercises to focus on your intention: quiet brainstorming and visualization.

- Hold one or more of the following crystals during this phase: fluorite, clear quartz, or sodalite.

Maintaining a Positive Vibration

- By maintaining a positive attitude by thinking positive thoughts, you are more likely to obtain what you want.

- Use the following exercises to maintain a positive vibration: affirmations and mini meditation.

- Hold one or more of the following crystals during this phase: clear quartz, emerald, citrine, pyrite, or sunstone.

Stating Your Intention

- It is time to state your intention. Continue to maintain your joy, gratitude, and positive energy. Refer to your brainstorming exercise to see what you chose for the number one item you wish to manifest at this time.

- Use the following exercises to state your intention: write and speak your intention clearly and be sure to keep it positive, to visualize your intention, and to meditate.

- Hold one or more of the following crystals during this phase: citrine, emerald, jade, clear quartz, tiger eye, pyrite, or green aventurine.
- Consider using the power trio: citrine, green aventurine, and pyrite.

Sending Blessings

- Sending blessings to all those who help our manifestation can continue the positive cycle of giving and receiving. When you send a blessing, you receive a blessing in return. You have sent your request to the universe to manifest, but the universe will send people to you to assist in some way. At first you may not know who you are sending blessings to, but as things progress, you can send blessings to those who help you along the way. Be sure to send them thanks as well.
- Use the following exercises to send blessings: make a list of all occupations that could be involved in some way with your manifestation request and send a silent blessing to all those who hold such occupations; when things begin to progress, send personal blessings to all who have helped your manifestation; send thanks to all those who have helped your request in some way.
- Hold a rose quartz during this phase.

Using an Abundance Grid

- Because you have already set your specific intention for manifestation, now is a good time to focus on abundance, prosperity, and money.
- Create your own abundance grid.

○ Write your intention on a sticky note or a small piece of paper that states, "I dedicate this grid to all that is positive and pure. I dedicate this grid to bring abundance and prosperity to myself and to all those who hold this space. So it is, it is so." You can change this statement to make it more personal, or you can use this one.

○ Use your intuition to help with this.

○ You will need a small clear quartz or selenite wand to direct the energy flow of the crystals.

○ Find a place to set the grid where it will not be disturbed by family, friends, or pets.

○ Print a grid template of the circle or infinity pattern, or any other pattern that stands out to you. You can find many on Pinterest.

○ Use the following crystals:

➤ Tumbled stones: citrine, emerald, jade, clear quartz, pyrite, tiger eye, or green aventurine

➤ Point for the center: clear quartz

What Happens Next?

Open and Allowing

• Be open and allow things to flow to you. If you try to control the outcome on your own, you may block the process. Let things flow.

• Use the following exercise to be open and allowing: quiet visualization—see yourself with open arms receiving your request.

• Hold one or more of the following crystals during this phase: labradorite or prehnite.

Trust and Believe

- It is important to trust and believe that your request has been received and that it will manifest. Let go and let the universe handle the details. When you know deep down within yourself, without a doubt that it will happen, then it will happen.

- Use the following exercise to help you trust and believe: quiet visualization time where you tell yourself that it is OK to trust and believe.

- Hold one more of the following crystals during this phase: amethyst, clear quartz, labradorite, or sodalite.

Signs and Indications

- Become aware of what is happening around you. Let yourself see the signs and indications that your request is manifesting. Recognize the guidance and direction being shown to you. Signs and indications can be aha moments, synchronicities, repetitive numbers or occurrences, or epiphanies. Sometimes they can be subtle or more straightforward, such as a phone call, email, or letter. The more you can increase your awareness, the more you will be aware of the signs and indications sent to you.

- Use the following exercise to help you see the signs and indications: spend fifteen to twenty minutes outdoors, close your eyes, listen to what you hear, open your eyes, look at what you see, and then journal everything you experienced.

- Hold one or more of the following crystals during this phase: clear quartz, selenite, sodalite, or labradorite.

Time and Patience

- Some requests take more time than others. It depends on the size of request, how it was stated, the emotional state you were in when you stated it, and if you have been able to maintain a positive vibration. You need to give the universe time to shift things in order to give you what you have asked for. Some requests can occur within days while other requests may take weeks, months, or even years to occur.

- Use the following exercise to help you with time and patience: quiet time to focus on being at peace, calm, and patient.

- Hold the following crystals during this phase: lepidolite, moonstone, selenite, angelite, or amethyst.

Acknowledgments

I am filled with gratitude to have created this book. I want to give my spirit guides, angels, and God my deepest gratitude. I am so grateful that I followed your guidance every step of the way.

Elisa Lee, thank you from the bottom of my heart for your continued support and amazing artwork. I look forward to many more projects together.

I wish to thank my friends and family who continue to support my crazy ideas and help me with all my endeavors.

I send my gratitude to all those who have contributed to my learning process.

My deepest heartfelt gratitude goes out to my Facebook fans, friends, and community members. You have touched my heart on the deepest level with your love and support. Thank you for being part of my journey, and I am humbled to be part of yours.

I thank everyone who was part of this project in some way, including everyone who purchased this book. It is my hope that you find something within these pages that helps you on your own journey. Thank you for your support.

I am so very grateful to be able to teach, write, and convey what spirit tells me to share.

Thank you!

About the Author

Debbie Hardy has had a close connection to crystal energy for many years. She facilitated her own physical, mental, and emotional healing and found a deeper spiritual connection by using crystals during meditation. Hardy is certified in crystal healing and angel therapy, and she is an advanced crystal master and a Reiki master. She's the author of *Meditation Made Easy Using Crystals* and *Spirit of the Crystal Ray*, and she has created several crystal-related courses available on Udemy. She enjoys spending time outdoors, taking photos, and relaxing in her Southern California home with her husband, daughter, and three dogs, Penny, JJ, and Emma.

Hardy hosts crystal workshops, meditation sessions, and discussions that connect people all over the world.

She invites you to visit her on
Facebook at facebook.com/dhardyacm1
Instagram @hardycrystalblessing
Website at www.hardycrystalblessing.com

Bibliography

Astrostyle.com. "Lion's Gate: The Sun and Sirius Sync Up to Open a Powerful Portal on 8-8." Felicia Bender. Accessed August 20, 2019. https://astrostyle.com/lions-gate-portal.

Hardy, Debbie. *Meditation Made Easy Using Crystals: A Guide for Using Crystals during Meditation to Heal Physical, Mental, and Emotional Issues and Deepen Spiritual Connection.* Charleston, SC: CreateSpace, 2017.

Hibiscus Moon Crystal Academy. "Crystals for Grounding, Prosperity, Drip Stone, and What Is Entrainment?" Hibiscus Moon. Accessed August 20, 2019. https://hibiscusmooncrystalacademy.com/grounding-prosperity.

Hibiscus Moon. *Crystal Grids: How and Why They Work: A Science-Based, Yet Practical Guide.* Charleston, SC: CreateSpace, 2011.

Fun Crystal Stuff

Would you like to join a positive spiritual community that focuses on crystals, angels, and spiritual growth? Join my Facebook page for weekly live events and crystal sales at facebook.com/dhardyacm1

If you would like to join a group of like-minded people on their spiritual path, my Facebook group, Crystalline Sage, is the place for you! This is a safe place where you can discuss your spiritual journey with others without judgment.

~

Did you know that I also have three crystal courses you can enroll in?
Visit www.Udemy.com, and search under my name (Debbie Hardy) or the courses listed below.

Exploring Basic Ways to Use Crystals for Your Well-Being

Amplify the Manifestation Process Using Crystals (This book aligns with this course)

Meditation Made Easy by Using Crystals (This course is aligned with my book Meditation Made Easy Using Crystals)

~

Visit my website, www.hardycrystalblessing.com, for more information on my distance-healing services. Sessions may include realignment of your energetic frequencies and/or removal of energetic blocks. This type of healing can promote good health in the physical, emotional, mental, and spiritual body. I use crystal energy, Reiki, and angel energy during the healing sessions.